JOURNEY TO
CHRISTMAS

Enjoy!

Judith P Foard-Giucastro

Journey to CHRISTMAS

A PERSONAL REFLECTION

JUDITH P. FOARD-GIUCASTRO

ILLUSTRATIONS BY MARJORIE WEEKS

SMALL BATCH BOOKS
AMHERST, MASSACHUSETTS

Printed in the United States of America

Designed by Megan Katsanevakis

Illustrations by Marjorie Weeks

Library of Congress Control Number: 2019916706

ISBN 978-1-951568-01-6

SMALL
BATCH
BOOKS

493 SOUTH PLEASANT STREET
AMHERST, MASSACHUSETTS 01002
413.230.3943

SMALLBATCHBOOKS.COM

Author's Note

*A*long time ago, when I was the mother of two school-aged children, I decided to keep a journal during the Christmas season of that year. It was November 1980, and I wanted to not only write about daily activities that in some way related to preparing for the holiday, but also to record my thoughts about the deeper spiritual meanings I found in the celebration of Christmas.

In January 1981, after all the celebrations were over and the decorations stored away, I compiled this small book based on my journal writings. After making attempts from time to time throughout the years to get the book published, I put my manuscript away and out of mind. Then, on Christmas Day 2014, I printed out a copy of my manuscript to show a friend and suddenly had the urge to make revisions and to try again to get it published.

So here it is, my Journey to Christmas. Some of the references may seem a bit dated, considering that the story is set in 1980, before so many of the technological advances of today. It is my hope, however, that the reflections on the true meaning of Christmas and ideas for ways in which to honor these remain relevant and inspirational to you today and tomorrow.

—*Judith Foard-Giucastro, July 2019*

Introduction

This is a story about the journey we make each year to Christmas. At one moment, it is taken with our hands, feet, and voices. At another, it proceeds through our thoughts, hopes, and inspirations. Sometimes the journey is over old terrain, memories of Christmases past. Other times it ventures onto new ground, the Christmas to come. Back and forth, from our actions to our thoughts, from Christmas past to Christmas present, the journey proceeds. Around us are the sights, the smells, the sounds, and the scenes of the season. We take them in. Some are discarded, for they would only lead us on a detour. Others are kept, to be reflected upon and to be savored. They become a part of what we take with us on the journey to Christmas.

November 30
THE FIRST DAY OF ADVENT

Advent is here! This afternoon the children put our Advent calendar on the dining room wall and placed four new candles on the table. After the evening meal, a candle was lit as the family shared in reading the first meditation of the season.

The worship service for this first Sunday of Advent also included the suggestion of a game of charades. Surprising how quickly the four of us—my husband, Larry; our son, Lawrence, age fourteen; our daughter, La Rue (an old family name), age ten; and I—became involved in this game. My husband came to the table patting his stomach and pretending to be laughing. La Rue knew right away that he was Santa Claus. Then La Rue pretended that she was riding a donkey (the kitchen stool) and we knew that she was Mary. I was next. I came to the table with a "sheep" (our fuzzy, white dog) following me. "A shepherd" was the immediate guess from the other three. Finally, my son, Lawrence, his lanky body seeming to extend halfway across the kitchen floor, came on all fours. "It's a donkey!" we shouted. The charades completed, we ended the service with a prayer and a few carols.

Yes, Advent is here again! Just a few days ago, as we celebrated Thanksgiving, Christmas seemed far off and strangely out of place. But now, the time has arrived to take the centerpiece of corn, pumpkin, and squash off the table and to put in its place the Advent candles. It is time to take the Thanksgiving decorations off the door and put up the Christmas wreath. It is time to take the big pumpkin from the porch and replace it with a tall, red candle and fresh boughs of evergreen. This, for me, will signify that Advent is upon us.

December 1

*N*o matter when Advent arrives or when the stores begin advertising their wares for the holidays, the Christmas season starts for me on December 1. When the month turns from November to December, I awake on that morning and say, "Today is December 1st. A special day has arrived!" December 1st has a freshness and a newness about it. The whole month lies ahead, and like a child, I dream of those magical days to come.

On December 1st, I know that it is time to begin that journey to Christmas. As with other journeys, I approach it with a mingled sense of joy and dread. There is reluctance at starting, and there is anxiety in thinking of all that lies ahead. But there is also excitement as I anticipate those unexpected moments of joy and delight that belong to the Christmas season.

December 1st—this is the day to begin planning for those customs that have become part of the family's traditional celebration. This is the day, perhaps, to put the gift list on paper or to bake the fruitcake that is stored away until Christmas week.

Most importantly, however, this is the day to start preparations for that journey of faith that will lead us to Christ's birth. As strange as it sounds, the search for the meaning of this event is akin to peeling an onion. We slowly peel the layers off, and as we do, we gradually discover those truths that belong to that whole mysterious act of the Incarnation. These discoveries that we make about Christ's coming are the most important part of our journey to Christmas.

So, let us look forward to this journey. Let us cast off that adult view of Christmas, the one that dreads the holidays as being too busy and too expensive, the one that nostalgically longs for the Christmases of childhood. Put on that childlike view of Christmas, that openness to surprise and delight in simple things, that ability to dream of magical things, and that capacity to wait expectantly for a wondrous happening.

Know that if you take on the spirit of a child as you make the spiritual journey to Christmas, you will be rewarded! As you think and pray, as you read and search the Scriptures for their meaning, and as you relive in your mind the first Christmas, you will come to a deeper understanding of this Divine event. Your preparation will bring you to that moment when your whole being is filled with the knowledge that Christ has come into the world and into your life.

December 3

On my way home from work today, I drove to a nearby town to purchase Christmas cards from a woman who was selling them for a charitable organization. The cards I chose are colorful, and they convey the message of Christ's birth in a simple but striking manner.

At times, my husband and I have talked of abandoning the practice of sending cards, but then we reconsider. We maintain this custom because Christmas is the only time of year that we correspond with many of our friends who live a great distance from us. Many of us have become involved in raising our children and pursuing our careers, and we rarely exchange personal letters during the year. At Christmas, though, we very much enjoy hearing from these friends whom we hardly ever see.

As I drove up the long road toward home just before dusk, a two-story Colonial home with candles in each window attracted my attention. Seeing it, I had the sudden realization that the Christmas season had arrived. I passed the house and traveled farther west toward home. The sun was setting, and the purple hills of the late afternoon were sharply silhouetted against a sky tinged with gold. The combination of the house decorated for Christmas and the faraway hills against the setting sun was beautiful. I said to myself, *Yes, it really is December, and Christmas is coming!*

December 4

The mild weather of the past few days has vanished, and, within the last day, it has become very cold and windy. The sky is a deep and cloudless blue, and there is still no sign of snow.

This morning I visited a woman who had recently suffered an incapacitating injury. Over tea, we enjoyed a leisurely conversation. Though we are of different generations, we realized as we talked that we have many of the same concerns about being a good parent. When I left, I knew that it would be difficult to say who had benefitted more from the visit.

Later today I went to the bank to cash my paycheck, the one that I had been holding on to as long as possible for purchasing many of the Christmas gifts. Soon I was at a department store to begin shopping. As I tried to make a decision on a toy for a toddler on the list, I felt a twinge of nostalgia thinking of my children, who were now past the age for the sturdy, colorful toys displayed on the shelf in front of me. At the checkout counter, I was pleased with the gifts that I had been able to find on this very first shopping trip of the season.

Christmas has inspired many great works of music. The experiences of listening to and performing these works are, for many, the means by which their journeys to Christmas are made. I remember a friend once saying, "Christmas would not be Christmas if I didn't go to a performance of *Messiah*." In Handel's *Messiah,* we find expression for our deepest religious yearnings and for our sense of wonder and praise at the birth of Jesus. Tonight I experienced these feelings as I listened to a well-known performer sing "O Holy Night" and "Gesù Bambino."

December 5

*T*oday was one of those very busy days. I was so occupied with the usual routine activities of life that I did not give much thought to Christmas at all. After work I hurried to the bank and to the store. By the time the groceries were unpacked, supper prepared, and the dishes washed, it was almost 10:00 p.m.

In our lives in the weeks before Christmas, there are often days like this one—days that are so hurried, we do not have time to think of anything besides the daily tasks that lie before us. I recall Christmas seasons when, day after day, I was so rushed that I would say to myself, *Oh, Christmas, don't come yet! I'm not ready. When you do get here, I hope I will be. For I need you, Christmas, to lift me, for just a while, above the incessant rat race. I need you, Christmas, to remind me again of the mission God has for me right now.*

December 6

*T*here is no snow, and again the temperatures have become milder. On this evening, Lawrence, La Rue, and I attended a local production of the musical *Godspell*. I had seen the play presented on television before and had played my record from the motion picture soundtrack many times. Even so, the message that this musical imparts still demands my attention. In the play, the difficult challenges that Jesus gave to His followers made me squirm in my seat. The musical reminds us that Jesus's call to us is as jarring as the sound of the alarm clock that awakens us in the morning, long before we are ready to rise. Jesus's call causes us to sit upright, awakened from a deep sleep, the alarm jangling uncomfortably in our ears.

It is when we hear that jangling that we discover again we have been making Christ into what *we* want Him to be for us. It is then that we realize we have fashioned

Him as our own, personalized Savior, perfectly tailored to our needs. In the midst of our Christmas celebrations, we must take care *not* to make Jesus into an innocuous figure, who is but an afterthought to add to our festivities!

December 7

*T*oday, on the second Sunday of Advent, Holy Communion was celebrated at the church. In the afternoon, my family attended the Christmas workshop, an annual event at the church. There were a variety of craft activities, ranging from very simple projects for young children to more complex ones offered to nimble-fingered youth and adults. The soft sculpture candle decorations, made from cloth and a filling, looked to me like a challenging activity, and indeed it was, for I spent all afternoon laboriously assembling my creation. The unfinished candle was taken home to be completed barely in time for Christmas. (Later, when we put up our tree, I hid the snagged edges of my candle in the large, thick needles of the evergreen!)

Early in the evening, many of us who attended the workshop went caroling. We went in good spirits, laughing and talking. The children who came along were excited and called to each other as they eagerly dashed to the doors of the homes of those on the caroling list.

In any given year, the people for whom we are singing are often suffering badly. There are those who are residents of nursing homes and have few relatives or friends. There are others who realize that this is their last Christmas. Some suffer anguish, for they have fallen on hard times. Our caroling may bring them back to memories of Christmases past, when they were well and family members were with them to celebrate the holidays. Several of the people to whom we sang looked as if they wanted most of all to have us to stay awhile to talk. When we left their homes, I wondered if we had left them with more pain than before, or had our singing raised their spirits?

Later in the evening, I learned of the sudden death of a person well known to my family. As I thought about the bad news I had just received, I could hear Christmas music in the background. *This joyful music of Christmas does not belong here; it is out of place,* I thought. Then I reminded myself that the tragic news and the Christmas music were not so incongruous after all, for doesn't pain and joy so often exist side by side in life? When are we *ever* able to sweep all sadness from our lives?

When I think of Christmases of years past, I find that many of them contained elements of sadness: a tragedy in the community, a natural disaster, the death or illness of a family member or friend, or a war that took many far away from their homes. At Christmastime, we cannot ignore these tragedies and pretend they do not exist. We must face the pain they bring and reach out to those who are suffering. In the midst of the sorrow that comes at this season, we must also affirm the Good News of Jesus's birth. No matter what happens, the news of Christ's coming cannot be muffled, and the joy of the season cannot be extinguished. Indeed, Christmas is a time of both greater pain and greater joy.

December 8–December 12

*C*hristmas is drawing nearer, and the pace of life quickens. Shopping for gifts can be one of the most dreaded experiences of this season. The crowded stores, a seemingly endless barrage of holiday advertisements, and our own concerns about having the time and money for Christmas shopping overwhelm much of the meaning of gift giving. There is probably no other Christmas custom that has been so perverted! What can we do to restore to the practice of giving gifts the meaning that is intended? Can we make our gift giving an outward expression of our gratitude for the great gift that God has given us?

One morning this week, I met with the minister at church to prepare a list of people to receive Christmas flowers this year. In the church there is the custom of decorating the sanctuary with poinsettias for the Sunday before Christmas. Each year, over one hundred plants are provided by parishioners in memory of friends and relatives. After the worship service that day, the poinsettias are delivered by the deaconesses to those who are ill and shut-in.

Nearly two weeks of December have passed, and there still is no snow. The snow that came in mid-November has already disappeared, and the ground is now hard and brown—not a pretty sight in December to New Englanders! In an area that is accustomed to snow in the winter, having snow before Christmas—no matter how much or how difficult to get about in—is a welcome event. Young people shout and dance about, and even the adults are known to act like excited children. In the days before Christmas, nothing can throw a classroom or even an office into pandemonium as quickly as that first shout, "It's snowing!" On December mornings when the snow is falling, those perpetual sleepyheads who usually must be dragged from their beds and constantly reminded to get ready for school are up at the crack of dawn and out sledding by eight!

One early evening this week, as my son, Lawrence, and I finished jogging around the neighborhood streets, we felt those first wet drops of snow on our noses. By the time we started to the store to buy groceries, a dusting of snow had covered the streets. "Goodbye, bare ground. I probably won't see you again until March, now that the first snow of December has begun," I said to myself.

After purchasing the groceries, we had a ten-mile trip to the railroad station to meet a weekend guest. The magic of snow before Christmas turned the trip, though somewhat treacherous, into a welcome adventure. Snow at night makes the streetlights fuzzy. Snow at night turns the lighted buildings of a city into dreamy castles. Snow at night transforms even a drab, vandalized railroad station into a place of enchanting beauty—especially when that snow comes before Christmas!

December 13

*T*oday was one of those typical busy Saturdays before Christmas. After the usual breakfast of pancakes, there were errands to run before making preparations for attending an evening Christmas party.

Shortly after seven o'clock, Larry and I drove to a nearby town for a progressive dinner held at the houses of several of my friends from work. Each home was very different and beautifully decorated for Christmas. The first, a cozy Cape Cod style, had the freshness and sparkle of a new home, and its occupants were happy to have friends come to see their first house. The second was a farmhouse, with its old-fashioned fireplace in the dining room and a Christmas tree full of children's decorations. This was a comfortable place for enjoying a delicious meal of lasagna and salad. Finally, it was out into the chill of night to travel to the last home for dessert. Upon entering this big old house through the double doors and away from the bitter cold, we welcomed the sight of the brilliant yellow glow from the fireplace in the dimly lit room. Gathered around the fire, we enjoyed dessert and laughed at the silly gifts and verses presented to each person for Christmas.

December 14

This Sunday morning, I awoke early to take my friend Ann to the railroad station to catch the nine o'clock train. She had spent most of the previous day visiting a prospective place of employment in our area. She arrived back at our home late last evening, and we stayed up awhile talking about our experiences of the day. With only a few hours of sleep, we were surprisingly wide-awake as we went to the train station. I returned home from the station in time to join the rest of the family for the Sunday morning service of worship at our church.

The afternoon was quiet and fitted perfectly my now sleepy mood. I undertook a small project of decorating a few places in the house for Christmas. Using some fresh greens, I decorated the mantel of the fireplace and put centerpieces on several tables.

This evening, when we conducted our third Sunday

Advent service, we used the figures from the Nativity set to tell the story of the angels' appearance to the shepherds. With the telling of the joyous story of the shepherds and seeing the Nativity set on the table, we realized that Christmas was now well on its way.

December 15

oday I shopped for gifts for Lawrence and La Rue. The stores were not crowded, and I had time to browse before selecting their gifts. As I drove home, I was happy to know that I was nearly finished with the Christmas shopping.

During the holiday season, we often become very irritable because we view the holiday in terms of tasks to be completed. We rush compulsively from one job to another, expecting to see in their completion our reward. Addressing cards, sending gifts, making cookies, planning a party, caroling, decorating the house, and on and on it goes. We tell ourselves that we have to do it because we have always done it for Christmas.

I wonder what our Christmas celebrations would be like if we eliminated or simplified those things that are a part of our holiday each year? Maybe our holiday calendars would benefit from some better planning. Think about it! Can we plan so that our days do not become filled with busyness? Can we plan our schedules in such a way that by the last few days before Christmas, we are indeed ready to receive into our hearts the news of Christ's coming?

December 16

*B*y now Christmas lights and trees are everywhere! In this area, electric candles and holiday wreaths of various sizes and designs are often used by homes and businesses for decorations. The clapboard house with candles in each window is as much a part of the New England landscape at Christmastime as the stately church spire or the red barn with a snow-covered roof.

A few years ago, the Christmas decorations in the business district of town were changed. Instead of the usual garlands and lights hung on the poles of the main street, colored lights were strung in the tall trees of the town green. The effect was striking! Townspeople enjoyed the new decorations so much that the lighting of the green became an annual affair. Workmen seen preparing the long strings of lights on a day in mid-November gave one the first hint that Christmas was on its way.

On a December evening, my family likes to make the trip downtown to see the lighted green. As we come down the hill and around the curve, it is not long before we catch our first glimpse of the many twinkling lights in the trees. In the background, too, we see our church, that elegant brick building with the lighted doorway and the graceful spire. What a sight to behold!

During the Christmas season, those passing the town green can enjoy these lights under a variety of conditions. In the gray dusk of a cloudy winter afternoon, their soft, dreamlike glow heralds the beginning of another evening. In the bitter cold, however, they are sharply bright, piercing the deep darkness of a winter night. When one walks beneath the canopy made by the sturdy trees of the green, the atmosphere is again quite different, for the warm glow of the lights creates more the mood of a summer carnival than that of Christmas. There are also those nights when the full moon rises over the northeastern corner of the church. Shining down on the lighted trees of the green, it too becomes a part of this colorful scene.

The lights on the green are the *most* fascinating, however, when it is snowing. As I walked along the main shopping street late one snowy afternoon, I saw the lights come on. The scene resembled a misty white curtain dotted here and there by shimmering orbs of red, yellow, and blue.

Then there was that unforgettable Christmas Eve when the snow was so blinding that the lighted trees could not be seen until one was within a block of the green. Later that evening, worshippers leaving the church after the eleven o'clock service were treated to a spectacular sight. From the narthex, as the church doors opened, we saw before us a heavy snow swirling about the trees, muting and blurring the colored lights on the branches. Listening to the crowd, one could hear exclamations of delight.

December 17

Today the snow sparkled under the sharply clear, blue sky of the December morning. In the afternoon, the golden sunlight cast long shadows across the snow, and all too soon the sun had set behind the distant hills.

Tonight it is very cold, and it is difficult to stay warm. In fact, I believe it is the coldest night that we have had so far this season. Nevertheless, in the evening, my family attended La Rue's Christmas concert at school. After the program, we traveled downtown to a restaurant for cake and ice cream, a special treat after the concert.

A trip down the long, straight road toward the center of town on an evening before Christmas is a delightful experience. One sees the soft glow of candles in the windows of the clapboard houses and the twinkling lights in the trees on the lawns. When a new snow covers the evergreens, the lights appear frosted, the red-, blue-, and golden-colored bulbs of the decorated trees shining faintly from beneath the snow-laden boughs, creating an enchanting illusion in the dark winter night. With new snow covering the roads, there is even more an air of a fantasy world, for the cars move ever so quietly down the streets, the usual sharp slap of their tires on the pavement mercifully muffled by the snow.

On our way to the restaurant, we passed the town green with its brightly lighted trees. Farther north, we came to another small green also decorated for Christmas. Near this park stands a beautiful brick Romanesque church. On its porch were two tall trees full of sparkling lights. To see all of this—the colorful lights on the green, the two slender trees at the entrance of the church, and the beautiful Romanesque church itself—was indeed a feast for the eyes!

Today I have been sensitive to the colors of Christmas. At the restaurant, even the reds and greens of a common holiday decoration seemed especially attractive. Earlier today I enjoyed looking at a card that had come in the mail, one showing white poinsettias, green holly leaves, and red berries against a dark red background. The intensity and the arrangement of the colors were very pleasing to the eye. I gazed at the card a long while before putting it on the dining room table for all the family to enjoy.

A meditation that I read this evening spoke of the gifts

of the senses.[1] The reading brought to mind the experiences of my day: the joy in seeing a New England town decorated for Christmas, the feeling of the sharp cold of the winter night, and the pleasure derived from seeing the bright colors of the season. The smells, the sights, the sounds, and the tastes of Christmas—how wonderful they are! They uplift the soul! They bring us joy! The senses are wonderful gifts from God!

December 18

*T*oday I saw both sides of Christmas—the frantic, busy side and the quiet, peaceful one. For all of those people who have the responsibility of making arrangements for the celebration of Christmas in the church, the days leading up to December 25 are hectic. At the church office, the phone rings constantly, and people are in and out of the office all day. There are many tasks to be completed and so little time left before Christmas!

The faster pulse, the knot in the stomach, and the tension headache are the burdens of those who perform the duties that enable all of us to celebrate Christmas in the church. This was the side of the season's preparation that I saw this morning at the church office as I completed arrangements for the delivery of the memorial poinsettias on the Sunday before Christmas.

Now, several hours later, I sit at my dining room table

in the absolute silence of the house for a few minutes before the children arrive home from school. This silence is the most beautiful music there is. The sun shines in the southern window, bringing warmth to a house chilled by the bitter cold of last evening. There is time to read the meditation for the day. The writer's comment, "A single Christian can be God's candle in a dark world," catches my attention.[2] What a sentence! How much it speaks of the despair of this world and of our mission in it.

The dark world can be the disillusionment of a person worn down by the cruelness of others. It can be the confident, happy child chided and bullied into self-doubting and shyness by his peers. It is the merchant of a small business giving up his store because he no longer finds satisfaction in a form of competition that has become too costly and too vicious. It is the harried receptionist taking upon herself the burdens of others and needing a few minutes alone to cry. It is the poor who suffer the first cold nights of December, wondering how they will buy fuel for all those winter days ahead. It is the young people of the inner city who despair in the lack of gainful employment and turn to drug dealing and prostitution. It is the suburban youth jaded by too much given too soon, seeking new thrills and new ways to consume. It is a political system grown cynical and doubtful about the dreams of justice and opportunity.

A single candle cannot light all the world, but as long as it bears witness to that light of Jesus Christ, it will not be extinguished. There will be at least some light in the darkness, and that light is our smile, our helping hand, our reassurance given someone, and our commitment to a just cause.

December 19

*T*oday is a clear, cold, and windy day. While at work, I went on an errand to a supermarket to price some foods for the children's Christmas party to be held at the daycare center I work at. At the store, I saw someone who brought to mind the thought I had yesterday about the world battering and kicking people about to the point that they become emotionally crippled. The individual I saw was a thin, pale, sad-looking youth who was shopping with a man and woman who were probably his parents. As the three of them went through the checkout line, the boy dutifully packed the groceries into bags. In a cautious and timid manner, he quietly shuffled out of the store carrying himself in such a way as if to say, "I am nobody!"

I looked at him and felt like crying. I wondered how he had come to be this way. Why did this boy, probably near the age of sixteen, already look as if he had been beaten down by the experiences of his life? I asked my-self, *What does Christ's coming into our world and taking upon Himself our sins and sufferings have to do with this boy? How do I put this scene and the good news of Christmas together?*

December 20

*D*espite the persistent efforts of our children to buy a tree at an earlier time, each year my family purchases our tree on the Saturday before Christmas. Agitation to change this date is especially increased in years when this day falls very near December 25. But my husband and I stand firm on our custom. Finally, "Christmas Tree Saturday" had arrived, and the weather was fit only for Arctic explorers to venture out of doors. The wind blew mercilessly across the snow on this frigid day. Unfortunately, there was no chance that a trip out to purchase a tree could be delayed with a mere five days left before Christmas!

We happily recalled past trips to the tree farm in the hills. This year was another story. We would not be going to our favorite place, as the farm's supply of Christmas trees had already been sold. How we would miss the trip up the winding dirt road to the hilltop farm. How we would miss seeing the rustic home that overlooked the rolling hills of pines and spruces.

Near the house at the farm was a small shed where we would select a saw and start our trek through the fields looking for a tree. I especially liked to take time in making the selection, for much of the joy of finding a tree, to me, was walking through the fields and admiring the beauty of the hills and trees. After choosing a tree, one of us would get down on all fours to slide the saw under the dense growth of branches to the trunk. Once the tree was cut, we would drag it down to the shed and pay the owner—a tall, ruddy-faced man with a friendly smile. After tying the tree on top of the car or stuffing it into the trunk, we would make our way down the winding road, content with our purchase.

Alas, this year would be different! After bundling ourselves in our heaviest clothing, we set out toward the northeastern corner of town, looking for a farm we'd heard had trees for sale. When we reached that farm, however, there were no signs that trees were being sold at all. We drove along several adjoining country roads searching for another Christmas tree farm, but our efforts were in vain. Finally, we realized that we would have to go to a roadside stand to buy a tree this year. Once back in town, we stopped at a large stand. After looking over the selection there, we decided that the prices were much too high.

Our next stop was at a nursery that had both live and cut trees. We considered buying a live tree that we could plant in our yard in the spring. At the nursery, prices were more reasonable, but the selection of remaining live trees was small. Moreover, the young man who assisted us said that a live tree could not be delivered to our house until Monday. Still, we examined both the live trees and the cut ones, and finally, the choice was narrowed to one live tree and one cut tree.

Two family members wanted the live one. "We will have a tree that we can plant, and it is not as wasteful as buying a cut one. They'll deliver it Monday, and we will have time to decorate it during the week. We won't have time to decorate it today anyway," they argued.

The other two protested, "But we don't want to wait any longer! Can't we get a cut tree that we can decorate today? These live trees are so small!" On and on the controversy raged, the supporters of each side throwing forth their best arguments, stopping only long enough to move inside the shop, for even the heat of the battle could not warm our freezing fingers and toes!

After a while, a decision was finally reached: It would be the cut tree, a prickly but very full-branched Scotch pine. We got out the ropes and the old, tattered red blanket that we had brought with us. The young clerk eagerly assisted us in tying the tree to the top of the car, no doubt relieved that we would soon be leaving.

Once the tree was tied securely enough to protect it from the brisk wind, Larry and the children all crowded into the back seat of the car. In my haste to assist with tying the tree onto the roof, I had tied the front door of the passenger side shut before anyone could get into the front seat! But we were finally prepared to leave. Our car must have been a strange sight slowly making its way through the center of town: The driver was alone in the front, and three good-sized persons were crammed into the back seat of the small car. All the while, the red blanket under the tree was flapping wildly down around the sides of the car windows. After the long, cold ordeal, we decided that the trimming of the tree had best wait until the next day.

December 21

*A*t church there are Sundays each year that are especially memorable. On these Sundays, there is an air of celebration in the congregation. The mood of the worshippers could best be described by the verses, "Enter His gates with thanksgiving, and His courts with praise." (Ps. 100:4)[3] The hymns, anthems, prayers, Scriptures, sermon, and even the decorations of the sanctuary all become the means through which the worshippers express their praise to God.

One of these special times is the last Sunday before Christmas. On that day, the church is filled with people. The singing is spirited, and the air is full of Christmas greetings given to one another. After the worship service, the deaconesses take the more than one hundred poinsettias that have decorated the sanctuary to people who are ill, bereaved, or shut-in.

On this Sunday, I helped to deliver the flowers. During my visits, I saw an elderly woman who would most likely spend Christmas in the hospital, a person who was seriously ill and confined to bed at home, and a member of the congregation whose parent had recently died. What would Christmas be like for them? Would it be more painful because they are facing sorrow at a time when they are "supposed" to be happy? Or would the message of Christ's coming, the caring shown them by others, or some other feature of the holiday give them some measure of support and comfort?

How do we celebrate Christmas in the midst of personal tragedy, disillusionment, or sorrow? Do we refrain from celebrations in those years that we suffer great hardships, or do we put up the tree and attempt to continue some of our usual observances, hoping to find Christ in the midst of our suffering? In those Christmas seasons when sorrow and anxiety are more a part of life than joy and expectation, is it possible that we might actually come closer to the discovery of the mystery of God's Incarnation? Could it be that in our deep despair, we might feel God reaching out to us, lifting us up and sustaining us? Jesus's coming would be only a Pollyanna event if He were not there, too, in those seasons when we are hurting deeply!

The sun had set and darkness was settling in over the countryside as I left the last house. Upon arriving home, I saw that my family had the tree up and ready to decorate. The long-awaited moment had arrived.

The large yellow box of decorations was brought from the basement, and my daughter, La Rue, excitedly unpacked it. As Larry and Lawrence tested the lights and arranged them on the tree, La Rue was placing decorations around the house. When the lights were in place, we began hanging the shining balls, the felt cutouts, and the painted wooden figures on the tree. Our ornaments come in various shapes, sizes, and materials, and each one has a story behind it. As we put the ornaments on the tree, we recalled some of these stories.

The branches of the Scotch pine were so full and prickly that some of the felt and paper ornaments were patted onto the tree rather than hung. Once the tree was full of ornaments, we wrapped the gold tinseled garlands around it. At last the tree was trimmed! We sat down to enjoy for the first time that unique treat of the Christmas season, the fully decorated tree. The small, sparkling white lights gave a warm, mellow glow to the darkened room. The lights caught the reds, golds, and blues on the shining ornaments that dangled from the deep green boughs of the fragrant pine. The room had indeed turned into a magical place!

December 22

What a busy day! Today was nonstop from 7:30 this morning until 9:30 in the evening. The day did not begin well. This morning, as three of us scurried around the house attempting to fit the usual morning preparations into an earlier time schedule, tempers flared, and we were irritable as we left the house on our ways to work and to school. I knew I had a long day ahead of me, and I was irritated that I had started the day off on the wrong foot. The drive to work, however, helped me to relax. By the time I arrived at my job, I was ready to finish preparations for the children's Christmas party to be held at the day care center in the evening.

This year the plans for the party were even bigger than before, for it was to be held in the evening, when most of the parents could attend. Parents were bringing food, and the teachers and children were putting on small plays. This day, the staff and the children were busy making the final preparations for the evening. The songs were practiced, the pageant was rehearsed, and in the afternoon, the large hall on the second floor was decorated.

By six o'clock, parents and children started arriving at the school, some having walked many blocks in the cold. Before long, the hall was filled with parents and relatives. The tables were overflowing with foods of all kinds: ham, pork, rice and beans, potato salad, cakes, ice cream, and soda. The children were dressed in their best clothes for this special occasion.

Soon the lights were dimmed, and the program began. The three-year-old children brought to the Christmas tree the decorations that they had made and hung them on the branches. Dressed in red paper Santa Claus hats and cotton mustaches, the four-year-old group sang several Christmas songs. Then the kindergarten class, in costume and with props, acted out "The Night Before Christmas," while their teacher read the poem. The program ended with a group of four-year-olds creating a Nativity scene.

Shortly after the children had returned to their chairs, Santa Claus entered the hall carrying a large pack on his back. The children screamed with delight. As they approached him to receive their stockings of small toys and candy, they looked amazed. Some children, their eyes remaining steadily on Santa, studied him in great detail: his suit, his beard, and his hat. All the while, they were strangely quiet as they tried to comprehend this magical figure.

Once the children had received their gifts, it was time to eat. Many of the foods on the tables were those served in Hispanic homes at Christmas. On this evening, people of different cultural backgrounds shared with each other their ways of celebrating Christmas. The plays and the songs were essentially those based on the customs that are observed here in the States. The foods were those often served in the homes of families from Puerto Rico.

By 8:30 most of the people had left. The teachers and staff were happy in knowing that the party had been greatly enjoyed by the children and their families. When we counted the chairs that were used, we realized that nearly one hundred and fifty people had attended the event. A day that was less than promising at its start had come to a happy conclusion.

December 23

*T*oday after completing my work and wishing my co-workers a Merry Christmas, I went to my car. The gray weather did little to dampen my spirits. Outside I heard the carillon from the nearby church playing carols. I thanked God for the satisfaction of projects completed and for the anticipation of the Christmas holiday to come.

On the way home, I stopped at a store to find the last gift on my shopping list, one for my son, Lawrence. I arrived home just in time to hide the game that I had bought him. When Lawrence and La Rue entered the house, they were full of excitement. No more school until January 5! On this gray December afternoon, warmth and cheer filled the house. The whole family could relax and enjoy the two days to come, Christmas Eve and Christmas Day. There was time to finish making the buttery

Austrian cookies and to take a ride about town in the evening to see the Christmas decorations and lights.

December 24
CHRISTMAS EVE

*I*t is one o'clock Christmas morning. The cold, blustery wind is whistling around the house and is driving freshly fallen snow into small drifts about the yard. Across the street, a light shines along the small path that runs through the forest of tall pines. The road by the house usually bustling with traffic is now deserted. I have just finished filling the stockings with candy and have placed the last gifts under the tree. Now everything is ready for Christmas. For a few minutes before retiring, I pause and think of the day that has just passed.

This Christmas Eve morning, I made a wreath for the front door using evergreen boughs taken from the tree. After completing it, the four of us went to town to buy the few groceries needed for Christmas dinner. That is when I became irritable. I did not want to be grouchy, for it was a special day to share with my family the Christmas preparations, but not until later in the day was I able to rid myself of my foul mood. Perhaps I was fussy because I was tired. Or was I fussy because I was expecting too much of Christmas Eve? At times, many of us try so hard to make a day like this special that we ruin it instead.

Often on Christmas Eve, I recall those of years' past. The feelings of excitement and expectation I had as a child on that day remain with me today. Even a trip to a store on the day before Christmas reminds me of those times in my childhood when I would buy gifts for my parents and my grandmother at the dime store in my town.

The setting of the sun and the lengthening of the shadows of late afternoon on Christmas Eve still bring forth the anticipation I had then when darkness fell on that day. I remember how my sister and I would look in wonderment as the tree was lighted at dusk on Christmas Eve. We would examine the wrapped gifts under the tree, shaking them, feeling them, and trying to imagine what could be inside those mysterious boxes. There was so much excitement in the air that we would be almost breathless. With the approach of darkness, the magic night had arrived, and Christmas morning was very, very near!

Now on Christmas Eve, I pause at dusk to take note of the coming of evening. If it has been a sunny day, I like to stand at the dining room window and watch the sun go slowly down behind the purple hills. If it has been cloudy, I like to sit in the living room and enjoy the soft glow the lights of the tree cast in the darkened room.

This year near four o'clock on Christmas Eve afternoon, a light snow began to fall. Having some leisure time before preparing the evening meal, I decided to go jogging. As I glided through the fresh dusting of snow, big flakes fell softly on my face, and the damp air was ever so soothing to my throat. My feet, bouncing up and down on the sidewalk, felt very light. Before long, the gray dreariness of the afternoon gently gave way to a sleepy, snowy dusk, and I was enveloped in its misty, white blanket. Passing the houses on each block, I could see the lights of Christmas trees and candles peering dreamily from the windows. With my attention so drawn by the beauty of the late afternoon snow, I completed my run easily.

Upon returning home, I was ready to prepare the evening meal. On Christmas Eve I serve foods that were traditional in my family growing up. Each year, on December 24, my father prepared oyster stew. How I loved his stew! The oysters in the buttery broth served with crackers and olives were so delicious! In the small Midwestern community in which I lived, oysters were a rare treat, for they were only available at Christmastime. Now the first taste of oyster stew on Christmas Eve brings me closer than anything else to those Christmas Eves of my childhood. As it was then, when only some of the family shared my father's enthusiasm for oyster stew, so it is the same with my family today. Larry and Lawrence do not like the stew. However, La Rue has come to enjoy it. She will be the one to carry on the oyster stew tradition.

For the evening meal on December 24, we put lighted candles on the table and used special placemats and napkins. The dinner consisted of oyster stew, clam chowder, oyster crackers, a relish plate, and Christmas cookies and fruitcake. After the evening meal, we went to the family worship service at our church held at 7:30. La Rue sang in the junior choir, and Lawrence assisted with the lighting for the Nativity scene that the junior high classes presented.

The second service on Christmas Eve is held at eleven o'clock, and it is one of those very special events of the church year. The sanctuary is filled with worshippers, some coming in large family groups. Many young people home from college or a job come together in small groups. Throughout the church one hears whispers of "Merry Christmas." There is a feeling of warmth that overcomes the cold of the late evening.

After the story of Jesus's birth is told through the reading of the Scriptures and music, the church is darkened. The candle lighters proceed from row to row lighting the candles of the worshippers, as "Silent Night" is sung by the congregation. Within a few minutes, the church is lighted by the glow of all the candles. The small, wavering yellow flames cast light even into the darkest corners of the sanctuary.

With the singing of "Silent Night" and the holding of the small flame in the midst of the darkened sanctuary, I reach one of the destinations in my journey to Christmas. In the singing of this song, I recall Christ's birth. I know that right here and now Christ is born again! I know that He is here with us! All that has gone before in the Advent season, all my actions and all my thoughts that were a part of the preparation, were for bringing me to this moment when I would experience in my heart again the birth of Christ, Emmanuel, God with us!

As the worshippers file silently out of the sanctuary, the silence is soon broken with the shouts of "Merry Christmas" to one to another. We experience a feeling of joy, a joy that we have discovered in that darkened sanctuary. The discovery is that Christ has come to us, and now it is Christmas Day!

And so it has been throughout the years. People from all over the world have developed these practices and have used these symbols that have enabled them to take part in the Incarnation event. For some, reenacting the birth of Jesus helps them to be a part of the Good News. For others, the symbol of a light shining in darkness gives them the confirmation that God is working out His purposes in the world. These are the means that enable Christians everywhere to complete their journey to Christmas.

Sometimes it can be difficult for us to find the Christmas message in the story of the Nativity. We have heard the second chapter of the Gospel of Luke read often enough that we could probably recite it from memory. Our response to the story can become mechanical, and the power of its message can be lost.

However, there is a part of us that expects more. There is a part of us that looks for something in that story that we have not seen before. Then at some moment, our eyes are opened and our ears hear! The message of the Nativity penetrates that shell that has grown around us, and it reaches our soul. We become like the shepherds who worshipped the newborn Christ and returned to their fields glorifying God.

Throughout the years there have been individuals who have helped us to better understand the message of Christ's birth. One such person was Saint Francis of Assisi. In 1224, he celebrated Mass before a real-life Nativity that he had a nobleman prepare. Saint Francis said, "For I would fain make a memorial of the Child who was born in Bethlehem, and in some sort behold with bodily eyes His infant hardships; how He lie on a manger in the hay, with the ox and the ass standing by." The story is told that as Saint Francis celebrated Mass, he was "overcome with tenderness and filled with wondrous joy." The many that had come that evening from the town and convents to the woodlands carrying lighted torches returned with joy to their homes.[4]

Throughout the ages, Christians have used religious drama, poetry, and song in their reenactment of the Nativity. Long ago in the Christmas dramas of England and France, through the portrayal of the shepherds, the common folk of the day were to identify more closely with the story of Jesus's birth. By means of a practice begun in the Middle Ages, people in Germany showed their devotion to the baby Jesus by the rocking of a cradle set in the church. The *Kindelwiegen*, as it was called, became very popular among the people, as did dancing around the cradle. Songs and poems from northern Europe tell of the long, dark night and the deep cold of the stable at Christ's birth. In this way, inhabitants of these northern climates could better understand the circumstances of Jesus's lowly birth.[5]

A few years ago, in a small Pennsylvania farm community, members of a rural church planned a real-life Nativity scene at the farm of one of the parishioners. I was one of those who walked with a flashlight quietly down the farm lane to the barn. There in the cold, dimly lighted barn, we were a part of the reenactment of Jesus's birth. Reenactment, retelling, and remembering the story of Christ's birth are ways that we participate in the wonder and joy of Christ's coming to earth to live among us.

Jesus as the light that shines in the darkness is a powerful symbol of the Incarnation. The first chapter of the Gospel of John uses the symbol of light to proclaim to us the Good News of Jesus. "In Him was life and the life was the light of men. The light shines in the darkness and the darkness has not overcome it." (John 1:4–5) "The true light that enlightens every man was coming into the world. . . . But to all who received Him, who believed in His name, He gave power to become children of God. . . . And the Word became flesh and dwelt among us, full of grace and truth; we have beheld His glory, glory as of the only Son from the Father." (John 1:9, 12, and 14)[6]

During the Christmas season, candles in windows, lighted trees, and candlelight services in churches are ways in which we proclaim the meaning of Christ's birth by use of the symbol of light. When I was a college student, I recall attending the candlelight service at a church near the school on the Sunday evening before Christmas. The church was dark except for the candles in the windows and on the altar. That evening, the pastor read from the first chapter of John. My understanding of the Christmas story was deepened as I added to that story the powerful symbol of Christ as the one who is the light for us in a darkened world.

Another experience also deepened my understanding of light as an important symbol of the Incarnation. It was December 1963, and the recent assassination of President Kennedy made the world seem very dark. I was in the first months of a new career as a social worker. My job brought me to homes where there was poverty. Each day on my way to the office, I passed streets of old brick row houses. During the gray, chilled days of late autumn, the houses looked even more forlorn than usual. I thought of the people who lived in those houses, and I thought of the people who lived in the concrete block apartments of the housing project where I often made calls. *Would life ever be better for them?* I wondered. I yearned for better times for these people, for more work opportunities, for less hatred, and less prejudice.

One early evening, as I left work and drove past the streets of drab row houses, a light fog covered the area. In many of the windows of these homes, there were already Christmas lights and electric candles in evidence, their yellows, reds, and blues muted by the fog and drizzles of the evening. By five o'clock, the skies were already dark, but the colorful lights shone through the windows of the row houses. These common things, electric candles and Christmas tree lights, shining through the windows of brick row houses had become sacred. The dime-store lights in the windows of row houses proclaimed that Christ had come to our world and that He had lived among us experiencing our sorrow and pain. In the midst of an impoverished neighborhood on one of dampest and grayest of December evenings, the fuller meaning of the word, Emmanuel, God with us, took shape in my mind. God is with us in our poverty, our despair, our darkness, and our hopelessness. His light shines in the darkness of this world, and because it does, our lights can shine in a troubled world, too.

Through song, poetry, and drama we can reenact the story of Jesus's birth. Through meditation on the symbol of light as presented in the first chapter of the Gospel of John, we can come to a better understanding of the Incarnation. These are ways by which we can proceed in our journey to the very heart of Christmas. These prac-tices can bring us to the throne of God in adoration and praise. We can draw close to God in prayer and can feel that sense of oneness and reconciliation to His purpose. In this way, we can reach our destination in the journey to Christmas.

It is past one o'clock in the morning, Christmas Day. The hour after returning from the late evening worship service is a time I especially enjoy. It is the time that Larry and I put the last of the children's gifts under the tree, get out the candy and the nuts, and finally sit down to enjoy together the quiet of the late evening.

Last year, this time was shared with my mother, who had come to spend her first Christmas with us in New England. What fun it was to have her take part in our celebrations! Years ago, she and my father had prepared the gifts and candy for my brothers, sister, and me. During her visit, she was again a part of this Christmas Eve ritual, helping me to do the same things for my children.

This year I am the only one who is still up, and I have just finished the gift wrapping and the filling of the stockings. I am sitting in the dimly lit living room looking at the tree and enjoying its beauty. I am thinking again about the birth of Jesus and its meaning. I am searching deeper, trying to understand more of this Divine Mystery. The wonderment of this time takes hold of me. I know that Christ has been reborn within me on this night! Christmas Day has arrived—a time for rejoicing.

December 25
CHRISTMAS DAY

*T*oday was the coldest Christmas that I can remember. Late last evening, the weather turned suddenly colder, and the snow was blown into drifts by the strong gusty winds. By morning all the windows in the house were completely covered by frost. The sun shining in the windows on the southern side of the house made many beautiful patterns on the glass panes. The day was so very cold that even the afternoon sun failed to melt the ice on the windows.

Lawrence and La Rue awoke at seven and slipped into the living room to see their gifts. Usually, they first come and ask if they can go to see their gifts. They know that we like to watch them as they enter the living room and see their presents under the tree. This year they must have decided that it was a hopeless cause to try to wake us. When we did awake, the first sound to fall on our ears was that of the grind and whir of the racetrack set. They had been up long enough to assemble the track and to get the cars running on it!

Soon after hearing the sounds of the race set, Larry and I were up and in the living room to enjoy the sight of the children playing with their gifts "from Santa." Later in the morning, after all the presents were opened, we laughed at the comical scene of La Rue donned in her striped nightgown and cap, a gift from her grandmother, sitting cross-legged on the floor, cranking the handle on the racetrack set as fast as she could.

Once Lawrence and La Rue have played with the gifts that they have received from us, they are ready to open the wrapped presents around the tree, those from relatives and friends. Someone volunteers to take the gifts from under the tree and distribute them. Before opening my gifts, I take note of the ones that La Rue opens as she rips apart the boxes so fast that the tags and gifts get mixed up. Later, as we write thank-you notes, we are not always sure that we are thanking people for the right gift! Lawrence, though, is a fanatical conservationist and opens the packages very carefully, trying to save as much of the wrapping and ribbons as he can.

Christmas breakfast is a simple meal usually of coffee cake or fruit stollen and grapefruit or oranges. Sometimes we eat after the children have had time to play awhile with their new toys and before opening the wrapped gifts. Other times we wait until after all the gifts are unwrapped.

The remaining hours of Christmas morning are spent looking over the gifts, trying on the new clothes received, and playing with the children. The floor is a mass of ribbons, wrapping paper, gift tags, boxes, toys, and instruction sheets. At some point, we stop to clean up, making sure that all the instructions and guarantees are kept and that no small gift is thrown out with the paper and the boxes. In order to keep Christmas morning a time to share together, we wait until early evening to eat the holiday meal.

After one of the meals on Christmas Day, we have a family worship service. The materials for it come from the Advent worship booklet that we receive each year at our church. In addition to the four candles that we have lit each Sunday in Advent, we now light the large white candle for Christmas Day. The words of the worship service remind us to celebrate the birth of Jesus in thankfulness and joy.

Often on Christmas Day, the radio is tuned to a station that carries a selection of Christmas carols or other works of the season. My husband and I especially like to hear Handel's *Messiah*. The pieces "For Unto Us a Child

Is Born" and "The Hallelujah Chorus" are ones that express better than any words the joy that we have because Christ has come to be our Savior.

When we experience this sense of celebration within our souls and tie it to our actions, Christmas can truly be a time for spiritual renewal. Our time spent with others on this day can have a special quality about it. The gifts that we give can be given out of a deep sense of gratitude, reflecting our thankfulness for the relationships we have with those persons receiving the gifts. Even the common act of preparing the meal takes on special meaning on Christmas Day. Extra care is taken to make the table beautiful and to prepare foods not regularly part of everyday meals. Surprisingly, fixing the larger dinner and cleaning up afterwards does not seem as onerous a task as one would think it would be. The spirit of the day makes the work seem light!

For the holiday meal served in the early evening, we set the table with linens or Christmas placemats and use our best dishes. We put candles on the table and serve foods usually eaten only at Thanksgiving and Christmas. Seated around the table in the evening, the candles flickering, the four of us are quieter than at most meals. Maybe it is the more formal setting of the table that has quieted the children, or maybe they are too tired after the long day of excitement for their usual chatter and joking? For my husband and me, we are enjoying the food too much to talk.

Once the Christmas dinner is over and the dishes washed, the darkness and cold of the winter evening settle in. All the special events of the day are over. Suddenly, we all are very sleepy. It is a relaxed sleepiness that feels good. We sit awhile longer, talking about the day, reading a little from a new book, or just looking at the tree with its sparkling lights. Lawrence and La Rue, very tired and knowing they want to be up early tomorrow to play with all the new toys, prepare for bed, offering little resistance. Larry and I stir ourselves for one last duty of the day, taking the dog for a walk. Outside, the night is quiet, and there are very few cars on the road. The streetlights pierce the deep cold and fall on the snow-drifted yard. Christmas Day is nearly over!

December 26

When I was a child, the day after Christmas was, in my estimation, the very worst day of the year! This was the day of "the big letdown." All the excitement that had been building the weeks before Christmas was suddenly gone. In my childhood, the first hints of the letdown to come began on Christmas morning after all the gifts had been opened. More of these feelings came as my family made the rounds from my grandmother's house to my cousins' house and opened gifts at each place. The letdown was eased somewhat if a gift from relatives out of town had not arrived by Christmas. My sister and I would comfort ourselves with the thought that there was still one more gift to open after Christmas was over.

By the time Christmas dinner was completed, dusk was on its way. The sun, low in the western sky, soon sank below the hills, leaving a purplish cast to the hills and fields.

The landscape of the late afternoon, quiet and subdued, mirrored my feelings. In my stomach, I had a sinking feeling when I thought of how fast Christmas Day had passed. Soon it was evening, bedtime, and the day was gone.

Then followed what was, in my mind, the most wretched day of the year, the day after Christmas. For me as a child, that day belonged with other infamous days such as that first day back to school after a vacation. The day after Christmas—let it be cold, windy, foggy, and damp, I would think, for that best fit my childhood mood on December 26. Remnants of those feelings still exist within me today, but over the years I have come to discover that the day after Christmas and those to follow have their own delights. These are days in which there is time to enjoy at a slower pace what remains of the Christmas holidays.

Today we made a trip to the home of Larry's sister and her family. We arrived in the late afternoon and shared with them a traditional holiday meal. This visit was for Lawrence, no doubt, the best Christmas gift of all, for he had the opportunity to use his uncle's computer. Soon after we arrived, Lawrence began working on the computer, and he stayed on it until midnight, stopping only to eat dinner. The next morning, he was up at seven o'clock and stayed at the computer until early afternoon, again taking a break only to eat!

December 27

In the early afternoon we began the second part of our trip, the five-hour drive farther south to the home of Larry's parents. It is an exciting moment when the car finally pulls into their driveway after a long trip. Lawrence and La Rue jump out of the car and race to the door, hoping to be the one who first sees a grandparent. After the luggage is carried upstairs, all of us have news to share and questions to ask. How was the trip? What has been happening in town recently? What have the children been doing? Then the beds are fixed for Lawrence and La Rue, and when Grandma asks them what they want for breakfast, the immediate reply is, "French toast!"

December 28

*L*awrence and La Rue were up very early, as is their habit when they visit their grandparents. They enjoy having breakfast alone with their grandparents. When Larry and I come downstairs, Larry's mother proudly tells us what the children have had breakfast. "Lawrence had four pieces of French toast and two glasses of juice," she says. "And then, when his grandfather came in to eat, Lawrence had another piece of toast. La Rue ate just as much—four pieces of toast." For the children, there is no breakfast that compares to their grandmother's French toast!

Later in the morning, we all attend church together and take Communion. At the church that Larry's parents attend, the Communion is served at the rail in front of the altar. Kneeling at the rail with the other members of my family to receive Holy Communion made clearer to me what I had often taken for granted: that those bonds to one another in our family are not only bonds of blood and of marriage but also those of our common faith in Christ.

December 29

*T*oday we made a sightseeing trip to several wildlife preserves. One summer we had come to one of these preserves on the Delaware Bay and had climbed the observation tower set in the middle of a marsh. La Rue had enjoyed the trip very much and wanted to return to this place in the winter. On this mild winter afternoon, we made our way over the boardwalk through the marsh to the tower that overlooks the bay and tidal creeks. Across a wide expanse of shallow water, we spotted a large flock of Canadian geese. At times a few geese would fly over the duck blinds on their way to join the flock. Hunters in the blinds raised their guns and fired, but with no success.

Immediately below the tower was vegetation common to this tidewater area. There was a heavy undergrowth of vines and also holly trees with their deep-green, shiny leaves and bright red berries. Here and there, high in the trees, we could see mistletoe spread over the bare branches. Along the Atlantic seacoast, the golden marsh grasses and the subdued green of the little thickets give the winter landscape a very different appearance than that of the interior sections of New England where we live. The Delaware Bay area has a beauty of its own with tidal creeks meandering through the long, tall golden grasses. Driving along the sandy roads by the marshland farms, there were large flocks of geese sitting in the cornfields. As we left the preserve, we saw, silhouetted against the gray sky of the late-winter afternoon, geese returning to a large pond.

In New England, the Christmas season, often very cold, is celebrated amidst red barns, snowy hills, and tall evergreens. How different it is here in Delaware! A part of the Christmas scene here in this coastal area is the damp air, wide expanses of farm and marshland, thickets containing holly trees and mistletoe, and old, brick Colonial-style houses.

Throughout the world, Christians are united at Christmas by the celebration of that central event, God coming to earth in human form. However, our observances of the holiday and even those images we carry in our minds to help us understand this event are greatly influenced by our surroundings.

December 30

This afternoon we visited friends who we had not seen for a long while. The couple, near the age of our parents, had been of great help to Larry and me when we were beginning our careers. They had been our elder counselors when we were on our own for the first time. Our afternoon visit was over all too quickly, for we had much news to share. As we left their home, they stood at the window, and we waved to them for as long as we could see them.

The trip to the rural community where our friends live was a nostalgic one, for my first teaching position had been in this area. I recalled bus trips down the small, deserted country roads when I was a coach and accompanied my girls' basketball team to games in tiny rural high schools.

Today the sky was a cloudless, soft blue, and the

landscape was a muted gold common to late December. Very few billboards or businesses dot the area of large fields that in summer produce a variety of delicious truck crops. Amidst the fields sit the narrow, two-story farmhouses and the outbuildings used for raising chickens, a major occupation of the area. The road, with its sandy shoulders, is very flat and straight, often going for miles without a curve.

In the late afternoon, as we return to Larry's parents from our trip, the landscape is golden and very still. Underneath the big, blue sky, the wide expanse of land with its occasional farmhouse moves slowly by me. My eyes are wide open, savoring it all.

December 31
NEW YEAR'S EVE

*L*ast evening, after returning from our day trip, we took Larry's parents to a restaurant for dinner to celebrate their wedding anniversary. This morning we prepared for the eight-hour trip back to western New England. After checking the house and the car one last time for all our belongings, we said goodbye, thanking Larry's parents for their hospitality, especially for all the French toast that Lawrence and La Rue had eaten! The weather was good for traveling, and we arrived home in time to get the cat and the dog from the kennel before closing time.

Even though it was New Year's Eve, I was the only one able to stay awake long enough to see in the New Year. All the rest, worn down by the eight-hour trip, were asleep long before midnight. The house was very quiet, and I read some, waiting for midnight to come. An article that I read in a magazine led me to reflect upon the holiday season that was coming to an end. I had begun Advent with a number of expectations: expectations for the pleasures that can be a part of Christmas, expectations for a greater understanding of the Incarnation, and expectations for a spiritual renewal. Tonight, when I thought about the past weeks, I knew that my expectations for Christmas, in large part, had been fulfilled. I felt ready to begin the New Year!

January 1
NEW YEAR'S DAY

*O*n this first day of the New Year, the weather was cloudy and cold. The house was very quiet, for my husband had gone to assist at a wedding, and Lawrence was ill. La Rue and I spent time designing new clothes for the paper dolls she had received for Christmas.

This evening we tried something new as a part of our holiday celebration—we had our evening meal on a blanket on the living room floor, picnic-style, around the Christmas tree. The food was kept simple, and we enjoyed this different kind of meal. While still seated on the floor, we used one of the last devotions in our Advent and Christmas worship booklet. The material contained questions about the year past and the one to come. Perhaps it was the informality of the meal or the quiet atmosphere around the tree that made this an especially good time for us to share our thoughts about the experiences of the past year.

We fondly remembered our summer trip to Montreal and Quebec. We talked of the concerns we had about our jobs and about school. As we recounted the events of the past year, I suddenly realized how much the family had been blessed. I thanked God for the experiences of the past year. Listening to some Christmas music, we enjoyed simply sitting there on the floor and talking.

January 2–January 5

The first days in January are days of readjustment, ones in which we return to the routines of our daily lives. Children and teachers go back to school, and factories and businesses resume their regular schedules. The last Christmas thank-you notes have been sent, and the gifts of clothing that were the wrong size have been exchanged.

In New England, the snow, which only a few weeks before was welcomed for Christmas, has begun to lose its charm. These early days of January can bring some of the coldest and snowiest weather of the entire season. New Englanders dig in, preparing for the hard winter days ahead.

Yes, these are trying days, for readjustment is painful. Readjustment to another routine is akin to stepping into the chilly water for the first swim of summer. It is akin to warming aching fingers and toes numbed by freezing weather. Children balk at having to rise early again on that first day back to school. There are butterflies in their stomachs as they return to their classrooms. Parents wish that they could hold on awhile longer to those vacation days when there was a little more leisure. Stay-at-home moms look forward to a quieter house but dread the post-season letdown. Workers feel strangely out of place in the familiar surroundings of the shop, factory, and office. Everywhere, people attempt to shift gears and to regain their direction.

In my home, routines begin to return to normal during the first days of January. The weekly trip to the grocery store is reinstated to its usual day, I return to work, and the children prepare for the first day back at school. At last, the first day of school after Christmas vacation had arrived, but, much to the joy of the children, school was canceled! This time it was not the childhood fantasy come true, the raging blizzard that closes school, but instead, a labor dispute that had rescued them from their awful fate. By evening, however, the dispute was settled, and the announcement was made that schools would reopen on January 6.

January 6
EPIPHANY

This is the last day of Christmas, January 6, the day of Epiphany. Christmas is an interesting phenomenon. When I think of carols, gifts, and all of the other trappings of the holiday in the middle of July, Christmas seems out of place and very far away. If someone sings the strains of a carol at another time of the year it is most likely done in jest. In the middle of summer, when I see the box of tree decorations in the basement, I do not feel the emotion that I have in December when I first open the box. In fact, the lights and all the other decorations in the box look rather ridiculous at any time of the year other than December.

Even as late as November 25, when someone says that it is only a month to Christmas, the day still seems far away. When Christmas catalogs begin arriving in

September, I have all good intentions to send in my order for cards by early November, but when that time arrives, Christmas is still one of the furthest things from my mind. The Christmas season, for me, starts in late November or on the first day of December. Even then, it takes time for me to become accustomed to the idea that Christmas is coming. By the week before December 25, however, Christmas is no longer out of place—it belongs! During the week after December 25, Christmas still lingers, and there is time to enjoy those waning days of the season. Then there is that one last day of Christmas, and that day is Epiphany, January 6.

Each year, we leave our tree up until January 6, and on that night we observe Epiphany by lighting the tree. This year we introduced another custom, one that goes back to Europe of the Middle Ages. The custom is that of having the *gâteau des rois*,[7] a cake that contains a bean. The person who finds the bean in his or her portion of the cake becomes "the king" or has the honor of selecting one to rule over the house for the evening.

After reviewing the recipes for an Epiphany cake and finding that I did not have the necessary ingredients, I improvised, making an orange cake and using a chocolate chip for the bean. When we were ready for dessert, I told the family about the custom of the "cake of kings." Unfortunately, no one found the "bean" in his or her piece of cake. Not until two days later, when we served the final portion of the cake, did we find the bean! It was in the very last piece served, my piece.

After finishing the meal, we used the worship service for January 6 found in our Advent and Christmas booklet. The meditation was about the observance of Epiphany, and we were reminded that even though the Christmas season is ending, "Christ is not put away. His presence is planted in our hearts once again to grow and blossom and bear good fruit this new year."[8]

Lawrence and La Rue each read one of the prayers. As a part of the service, family members were asked to share feelings about the season's coming to an end. We found ouselves expressing thoughts that in the course of busy days we often neglect to share with each other. Two of us said that we were reluctant to put Christmas behind us and to take down the tree and decorations, but we said that we felt ready to move ahead to find new challenges in the year ahead. Lawrence ended the discussion by saying that he was sad that Christmas vacation was over, and he had to return "to dumb old school."

In the United States, Epiphany is not as important a holiday as it is in some parts of the world. Even so, today I heard a program of music on the radio for the Epiphany season, and there were also several announcements of Epiphany day parties being given in the area. At my church on Epiphany Sunday, the story of the three kings is recounted, and the figures of the wise men are put in the crèche that sits at the front of the church. Epiphany is the season in which the church remembers that Jesus's message is to all people. It is the time in which we reaffirm our mission.

There is no better way to leave Christmas than this! In Advent we prepare for Christ's coming. At Christmas He comes and is reborn in us. He lifts us out of our despair and offers to be our guide throughout our earthly trek. He gives us a vision of what our lives can be and what our mission is. During the Christmas season, we have felt alive, and our senses have been treated to a banquet of beautiful sights, delicious smells, delightful sounds, and warm touches.

Now we leave Christmas more convinced than ever that Jesus is the Light of the World and that He has given us light to share with others. Now we are as the shepherds, running abroad to tell the Good News. We are as the wise men, returning joyous to their homeland after that special journey in search of the Christ child.

Even though January in this northerly climate is bitterly cold and snowy, it is the time in which I often feel a renewed spark within me and am willing to accept new challenges and begin new projects. Over the years, I have slowly come to realize that despite the harsh weather, January is a good month. I have learned that after a few days of "the Christmas letdown," I feel a resurgence of energy and a renewed spirit.

Maybe that resurgence of energy and that renewal of spirit are signs that the journey to Christmas—its preparation, its arrival, and its completion—can bring an uplifting of the soul.

This uplifting carries us back into our everyday world rejoicing and sharing with others the light of Christ's life. This light of Christ is seen in our words and actions. It is also seen in the sparkle in our eyes and the smile on our lips, which tell others that there are reasons for hope and joy in this life.

The journey to Christmas has ended. We are back home and back to our familiar routines, but we are different, for we have made this important journey.

Afterword
JANUARY 10

This afternoon we took down the Christmas tree. It had sat there in the corner of the living room, hardly noticed by us since Epiphany, its magic having vanished. The big yellow packing box was brought from the basement. One last time, we turned on the lights and put on a record of carols, but it was not the same. La Rue went throughout the house collecting the decorations in each room, bringing them to the living room for sorting and boxing. Then we gingerly removed the ornaments from the prickly branches of the Scotch pine. Once that was completed, the garland was taken off the tree and wound around a piece of cardboard. At last the lights were turned off and carefully taken from the tree. The storage box was packed and carried to its place in the basement.

Finally, Larry and Lawrence lifted the tree from its

stand and carried it to the corner of the backyard. With that, the last act of Christmas was completed. Now the tree rests in the midst of a pile of leaves and old tree branches, a place of shelter and food for small animals and birds during the cold winter days ahead.

Epilogue

As I prepared my journal of nearly forty years ago for publication, I found it comforting, as an elderly widow, to look back at that couple in the prime of life rearing their two children. There we were, the four of us, under one roof coping with everyday issues, no less at Christmastime, but also finding pleasure in our life together. I derive satisfaction, too, knowing that the children of those days have become responsible and loving adults.

In several entries of my journal, I brought up the question, how does one deal with tragedy and grief at a time of the year that is supposed to be joyous? In the past decade, I have been thrust into the midst of this dilemma. Both of my late husbands passed away during the Christmas season. As I went through those difficult times, I wondered if I would ever be able to celebrate Christmas again.

Surprisingly, though, I discovered that Christmas, with all of its customs, rituals, and spiritual meanings, was comforting even in the midst of my grief. The music, lights, and pretty decorations brought beauty and calm to my soul. In family gatherings, I found the support of others and felt less isolation. The religious services brought structure and gave me direction for what lay ahead.

Christmas, I realized, was something more powerful than the events that had brought tragedy into my life. Christmas celebrates God sending His son, Emmanuel, to earth. Emmanuel means "God with Us"—God with us not only in joy but also in sorrow.

ENDNOTES

1. "God's Gift of Our Senses," by Margaret Buell Allen in *These Days*, Larry M. Correu, Editor, Vol. 10, No. 6.

2. "Our Gift to God," by Margaret Buell Allen in *These Days,* Larry M. Correu, Editor, Vol. 10, No. 6.

3. *The New Oxford Annotated Bible*, New Revised Standard Version. New York: Oxford University Press, 1991.

4. *Christmas Customs and Traditions*, by Clement A. Miles, New York: Dover Publications, 1976, pp. 105–106.

5. *Christmas Customs and Traditions*, by Clement S. Miles, New York: Dover Publications, 1976, pp. 108–109.

6. *The Holy Bible*, Revised Standard Version, Second Edition. Dallas, Texas: The Melton Book Company, 1971.

7. For more information about this custom see *Christmas Customs and Traditions*, by Clement A. Miles, New York: Dover Publications, 1976, p. 340.

8. Every year, our Christian education director, Dorothy Moore, gave each family a booklet to use during Advent and Christmas. I believe she made them herself, possibly drawing on worship resources.

About the Author

*J*udith P. Foard-Giucastro, a native of Missouri, is a retired teacher and social worker. After retiring, she published her first YA novel, entitled *Senior Year*. Previously, she has written meditations for the devotional magazine *These Days*, as well as a history for the book honoring the three hundredth anniversary of First Congregational Church of Westfield, Massachusetts, where she now lives.

In 2017, Foard-Giucastro published, with her late husband Giuseppe Giucastro, a book entitled *Another Face of God*.

CPSIA information can be obtained
at www.ICGtesting.com
Printed in the USA
FSHW021343091119